Contents

LIBRARIES NI
WITHDRAWN FROM STOCK

CHAPTER 1

Why does my cat do that?

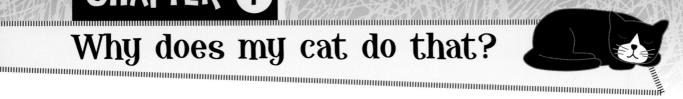

Your cat follows you into the kitchen. She pads along behind you and attacks your heels. You reach down to stroke her. Is she asking for some attention? She looks up at you and almost closes her eyes while you touch her. She likes this!

You turn and walk towards the sink. You're thirsty. On goes the cold water. Your cat leaps onto the worktop. Her head dips under the tap to catch the final drips. You turn off the tap. She looks at you with pleading eyes. On goes the tap with a slow drip now. Your cat drinks from the tap. She doesn't seem to mind when her fur gets wet. She stays there until she's satisfied. This has happened before. It's just one of your cat's fascinating behaviours!

Have you wondered why cats act the way they do? People who study cats have decoded some of these mysterious behaviours to help us understand our feline friends. If you know a cat, see if you can work out what it's trying to tell you!

Did you know?

Have you ever seen cats hanging around together? A group of cats is called a clowder.

Cats have habits just like we do. They can be odd or funny or helpful.

Cats use their senses to understand the world. You can use your senses of sight and hearing to get to know cats. It may take time, but it will help you to understand what cats are trying to communicate.

Mood clues

Cats' faces aren't as expressive as dogs' faces. Cats can blink their eyes, yawn or show their teeth. But their facial expression doesn't change much. To understand what a cat is feeling, watch its body signals. Ear position gives information on a cat's mood:

	Ears forward with half-closed eyes	The cat is content.
	Twitchy ears	The cat is unsure of its feelings.
	Folded-down ears	The cat is afraid.
	Ears jutting forward	The cat is curious and wants to hear well.
	Ears curled back while whiskers are forward	The cat is angry.

A cat's tail also gives clues to its mood:

	The tail fur is puffy	The cat is angry or frightened.
	An upright tail with flat fur	The cat is curious or happy.
	A tail hanging low or between the legs	The cat is insecure or anxious.
	A quivering tail standing straight up	The cat is happy or excited.
	The tail is thrashing back and forth	The cat is upset; the faster the tail moves, the more upset the cat is.

 ## Scents make sense

Cats also communicate using scent. When a cat knows another cat well, they'll touch noses. This is a way for cats to show they recognize each other.

Marking allows a cat to leave a message for other cats that come into their territory. Cats mark territory with scent by rubbing against items with their cheeks and **flanks**. Cats have scent glands in these areas. The scent stays on the object and tells other cats to stay away. Cats mark humans in the same way.

A cat may mark its territory around your house and garden.

If you've been around a cat, you may have noticed it make a strange face after sniffing something. Smell is so important to cats that they have an extra **olfactory** organ called the Jacobson's organ. It's in the roof of a cat's mouth but is connected to its nose. When a cat smells something unusual, it will sniff it. The cat then opens its mouth to let the scent flow over the Jacobson's organ. It gives the cat more information about where the scent came from.

Cats often use their Jacobson's organ when smelling other cats.

Did you know?
Cats have 200 million scent receptors, compared to 5 million in humans. Cats can smell where and with whom you've been!

flank part of a cat's body between the bottom rib and the hip
olfactory relating to the sense of smell

Did you know?
Cats that aren't tame rarely miaow. Experts believe that pet cats miaow to communicate with their owners.

 ## Cat sounds

Cats can make more than 100 different sounds. The classic miaow is the one cats use most. But miaows can sound different from one another and have different meanings. A soft miaow might be the way a cat greets its owner. A loud miaow can be a demand for food. A high-pitched miaow could mean the cat doesn't want to be touched. Cats learn how owners react to specific sounds. They change the sound of their miaow to get what they need.

10

Purring is the sound of a happy cat. Or is it? Scientists aren't sure. Cats purr when they are snuggled on a lap. Cats also purr when they are injured, sick or anxious. A purr may be a way for a cat to comfort itself. Perhaps one day this purr-fect mystery will be solved.

Purring is a common cat sound but the least understood.

Narrowing of the eyes and slow blinking is sometimes called a "kitty kiss".

Blink those eyes

When a cat blinks and narrows its eyes at another cat, scientists believe it is sending a feline message of friendship. Cats can also give humans this sign of affection, and humans can return the love. Try to make friends with a cat. Gaze at it. Slowly blink. See if the cat blinks back at you.

Did you know?

The oldest living **domestic** cat in the world lived to be 38 years old. Crème Puff lived in Texas, USA, and died in 2005. The average lifespan of an indoor cat is 15 years.

Chatty cats

Some cat breeds don't miaow much, but others have a lot to say. Siamese cats are the most vocal breed. They can imitate a human baby's cry. This cat will always tell its owner what it needs and when. But its high-pitched miaow can be annoying!

The Tonkinese cat loves to greet visitors at the door to talk non-stop in its friendly voice. This cat also has a powerfully loud purr.

The large, long-haired Maine Coon cat talks to people in a melodic, chirpy voice. The Maine Coon's chatter can sound like it's asking questions because of the rising tone at the end.

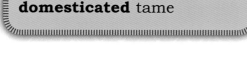

domesticated tame

CHAPTER 2
Cat behaviour and humans

Cats have lived with humans for thousands of years. But people sometimes consider cats to be selfish and distant. Is it true? Or are they just self-reliant?

Why does my cat ignore me?

Some cats are friendly and others are timid. A cat's personality depends a great deal on its **genes** and the early experiences it has as a kitten. If a kitten has been cuddled and taught how to play by its mother, the adult cat will often be friendly.

A cat ignoring its owner may just be a sign of its independent nature.

Cats that behave like dogs

Abyssinian, Burmese and Manx cats each have qualities that are similar to dogs. Many Abyssinian cats love water. They play fetch and want to be involved in whatever their owners are doing. They can even be trained to walk on a lead. Burmese cats are friendly cuddlers. They like to play with children and follow their owners around. Manx cats are friendly and affectionate. They love to be around people. These cats can be trained to answer commands such as "come" and "no".

Most cats don't need as much attention as dogs. A cat's wild **ancestors** lived and hunted alone. Some of that wild independence still exists in domestic cats. Dogs are different. They are pack animals and need to be with humans or other dogs to be happy.

gene part of every cell that carries physical and behavioural information passed from parents to offspring
ancestor member of an animal's family who lived a long time ago

15

A cat in your lap

Has a cat ever jumped into your lap and started purring and **kneading** its paws? Why in the world does it do this? It's repeating happy behaviour from when it was a kitten. Kittens knead their mother's skin to get the milk flowing. If a cat is kneading you with its paws, it usually means that it's very happy.

When a cat leaps into your lap and begins to snuggle, it's one of the friendly behaviours a cat displays to communicate pleasure. It's saying it wants to be friends.

knead push up and down with the paws

Sitting or laying on your lap makes a cat feel warm and safe.

 ## Don't touch me!

What is a cat communicating if it won't let you pick it up? It may mean the cat is sensitive to having its tail or spine touched. Or perhaps it doesn't like cuddling. Pay attention. Cats tell us what they like or don't like in very firm ways. A usually happy cat that starts biting or scratching when its belly is rubbed is telling you to stop – now! The belly is a sensitive area for many cats. Touching it can make them feel uncomfortable.

Ball toys mimic the movement of small mice – something cats love to chase!

 Bad habits

Cats like to chew on objects that have different textures. Chewing on power cables, plastic or metal blinds or fabric can be dangerous. Cats will sometimes chew if they're feeling bored or stressed. Help your cat release its boredom by providing toys for chewing.

Did you know?

Cats spend one-third of their lives grooming themselves. This natural behaviour keeps them clean, healthy and comfortable.

Some cats may eat non-foods, such as fabric or elastic bands. This behaviour is called **pica**. It may begin at a stressful time in a cat's life, such as when it moves to a new home or its owners get another pet. To discourage pica, play with your cat often and keep non-food items your cat wants to eat stored away. Also check with your vet to make sure your cat doesn't have any medical problems that are causing the pica.

Playing with your cat regularly could prevent pica.

pica urge to eat things that aren't food

CHAPTER 3

The hunter cat

You feed your cat every day. But cats are hunters at heart. Before cats were bred to be pets, they lived independently in the wild. They hunted for food and protected themselves. Many domestic cats display hunting behaviours passed down from their ancestors.

Hunting play

The cat crouches around the corner of the kitchen. Human footsteps come close. The cat gets very low to the ground. The human walks by. The cat pounces on the person's feet. The human runs. The cat chases and nips at the person's heels. The cat is showing hunting behaviour.

Domestic cats mimic hunting behaviour indoors by first hiding and then pouncing on an object.

Moving things attract a cat to pounce and play. A crumpled piece of paper batted around is like an active game of mouse-hunting for a cat. A piece of string moving up and down might catch a cat's attention. The cat waits with its claws out to strike at its "**prey**". A laser pointer dot moving around a dark wall may make a cat go into hunting mode. People using knitting needles or pencils can cause a cat to follow the motions and use its hunting skills.

prey animal hunted by another animal for food

From high up, cats are able to observe their territory.

Up high and tucked in

Many cats climb up on top of bookcases or other high places. From this view, a cat watches all that is happening from a safe place. But it isn't always safe – be watchful of where your cat climbs.

Have you ever seen a cat turn a box on its side and squeeze inside? Cats like to "own" small spaces and hide from us. It makes them feel safe and secure. When a cat is anxious, hiding is a way to gather confidence.

Thanks very much!

When cats bring home a dead mouse, most owners think it's a gift. But recently scientists have said this isn't the case. It's natural for cats to hunt. When they catch prey, their **instincts** tell them to return home with it. Experts think domestic cats forget they don't need to hunt until they walk through the door. So they drop the prey on the floor.

Did you know?

Have you ever found your cat sleeping on a pile of dirty washing? Cats find their owner's scent comforting — just like their mother's scent was comforting to them as kittens.

instinct behaviour that is natural rather than learned

CHAPTER 4

Mysterious behaviours and abilities

Be careful about stroking your cat after it has smelled catnip until you know how it will respond.

Some things cats do continue to mystify animal experts. These are the behaviours that cat owners love to tell stories about. In some cases, experts think they can explain parts of odd behaviours, but other parts aren't yet fully understood.

Catnip

Catnip can bring out a variety of behaviours in a cat. This herb can cause a cat to feel happy. A cat might flip and twist its body on the floor after sniffing catnip. But the scent makes some cats growl, run around the house or become very protective of their toys. Scientists aren't sure, but they think that the oils in catnip stimulate a cat's brain and cause these behaviours.

Some experts think cats have a sixth sense when finding their way home.

 Going home

Many true stories exist of both wild and domestic cats finding their way home over hundreds of miles. How? It may be an extra-developed sense of time and direction. Some people say these cats use the sun and stars to find their way home. Or they use their memory to guide them back to their owners. Scientists aren't exactly sure about this built-in sense of navigation. It's another example of amazing cat behaviour that needs to be studied.

There are many universities that now study both domestic cat and wildcat behaviour.

 ## Learning about cats

A cat's behaviour may be simple to understand or very strange. Cats still carry many traits from their wild ancestors. Their actions both entertain and mystify us. Science has already given us some answers to their puzzling behaviours. Perhaps future research will give us an even better understanding of our feline friends.

A hero called Pudding

The night Amy Jung brought her cat Pudding home won't be forgotten. In February 2012 Amy adopted Pudding from an animal shelter in Wisconsin, USA.

That night Amy, who has **diabetes**, had a **seizure** in her sleep. Pudding sat on Amy's chest and swatted at her face. Amy woke up and shouted to her son, Ethan. But Ethan didn't hear her. So Pudding bounced on Ethan's bed until he woke up. Ethan called for help. Amy survived, and Pudding was a hero! Pudding is now a therapy cat. His most important job is to sit at Amy's feet and miaow when he senses her blood sugar is low.

diabetes condition in which there is too much sugar in the blood
seizure sudden attack that causes a person to lose consciousness

Teach your cat to do tricks

How about teaching your cat a few tricks? Cats are more motivated by play, but a treat and lots of praise will help. They also need lots of chances to practise the trick. Start with something simple and have patience.

 Shaking hands

Even an older cat can master this trick. Teach for only 10 minutes at a time. Always do it before a meal at the same time each day.

1. While your cat is sitting still, gently grasp one paw in your hand. Hold a treat in your other hand.

2. Gently move the paw you're holding up and down, as if you're shaking hands. Release your hold on the paw but push it up in the air. When the paw comes back down into your hand, grasp it and say your cat's name and "shake".

3. Immediately reward your cat with a treat and say, "Good shake".

4. Repeat this lesson again. If the cat begins to raise a paw on his own, give it an extra treat.

Jumping through hoops

This trick requires a training device called a clicker and a hula hoop toy. You can buy a clicker from a pet shop or online. Train your cat to connect the sound of the clicker with receiving a treat. Click-treat-repeat. Do this several times. Soon your cat will be ready to do this fun trick.

1. Hold the hula hoop on the ground between you and the cat. Sit in front of the hoop holding the clicker and a treat.

2. Click and offer the treat after the cat walks over the hoop to your side.

3. With more practice, you can speed up the clicker or lift the hoop off the ground and see if your cat will jump through it.

4. Get a friend to help you and try teaching your cat to jump through two hoops.

Glossary

ancestor member of an animal's family who lived a long time ago

diabetes condition in which there is too much sugar in the blood

domesticated tame

flank part of a cat's body between the bottom rib and the hip

gene part of every cell that carries physical and behavioural information passed from parents to offspring

instinct behaviour that is natural rather than learned

knead push up and down with the paws

olfactory relating to the sense of smell

pica urge to eat things that aren't food

prey animal hunted by another animal for food

seizure sudden attack that causes a person to lose consciousness

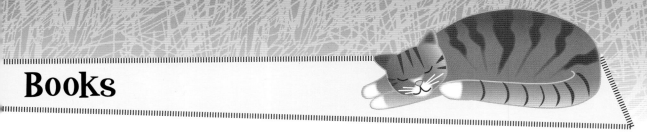

Books

Care for your Kitten (RSPCA Pet Guide), RSPCA (HarperCollins, 2015)

Caring for Cats and Kittens, (Battersea Dogs & Cats Home Pet Care Guides), Ben Hubbard (Franklin Watts, 2015)

The Cat Encyclopedia (DK Cats), DK (Dorling Kindersley, 2014)

Cats (Animal Family Albums), Charlotte Guillain (Raintree, 2013)

 Websites

www.cats.org.uk/cat-care/cats-for-kids

Find out some fascinating feline facts, take part in fun activities and games and get useful cat care advice.

www.rspca.org.uk/adviceandwelfare/pets/cats

Find out more about cat behaviour.

Comprehension questions

1. Why do scientists think cats touch noses?

2. Looking at the information in this book, find two ways that cats are different from dogs. Can you find any other examples using books or online resources?

3. Look at the picture on page 7. How do you think the cat is feeling? Give two reasons that support your answer.

Index